T0077030

RICHARD DANIELPOUR

PIANO FANTASY
("Wenn ich einmal soll scheiden")

FOR SOLO PIANO

Commissioned by the Gilmore International Keyboard Festival
for Gilmore Young Artist, Adam Golka

The first performance was given by Adam Golka
on 31 July 2009, in Lombard, Il.,
at the National Conference on Keyboard Pedagogy

AMP 8299
First Printing: June 2016
ISBN: 978-1-4950-6202-5

Associated Music Publishers, Inc.

DISTRIBUTED BY

7777 W. BLUEMOUND RD. P.O. BOX 13819 MILWAUKEE, WI 53213

Composer's Note

My *Piano Fantasy* was composed in the summer of 2008 on a commission from the Gilmore Foundation for their young prizewinner that year, Adam Golka. I had heard Adam play at a retrospective concert of various works of mine in 2007 in Fort Worth. I was so impressed by his playing that I told him that at some point I would eventually want to write a virtuoso solo piano work for him. Noticing his interest, I began thinking about the proposed work in the spring of 2008. During that time I was listening again to a recording of the Bach *St. Matthew Passion*, the monolithic oratorio which had a great deal of influence on my decision to become a composer at the age of 16. Upon hearing the work again for the first time in several years, I was particularly struck by the final chorale ("Wenn ich einmal soll scheiden") which is a setting of the well-known Lutheran chorale "O Haupt Von Blut und Wunden," in the Phrygian mode. I decided early on in the process to quote the chorale note for note at the end of the work, and in doing so, create the effect of a set of free variations in reverse — in which the theme appears at the very end of the piece.

Piano Fantasy is dedicated to my friend of 25 years, Dr. James Cross.

—Richard Danielpour

Duration ca. 16 minutes

Information on Richard Danielpour and his music may be found on:
www.musicsalesclassical.com
www.richard-danielpour.com

to Dr. James Cross

PIANO FANTASY
("Wenn ich einmal soll scheiden")

Richard Danielpour
(2008)

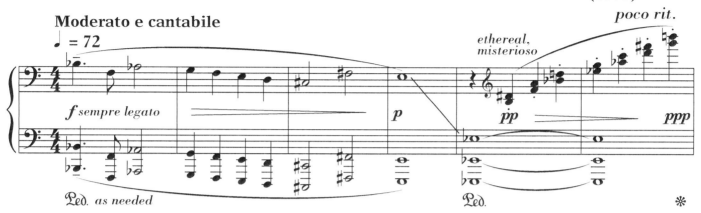

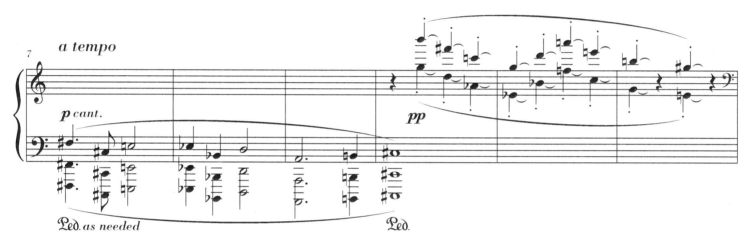

*: Grace notes before the beat

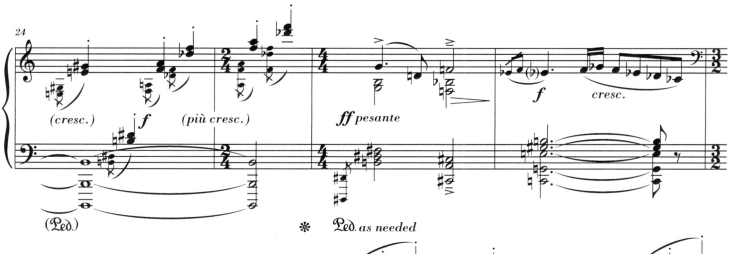

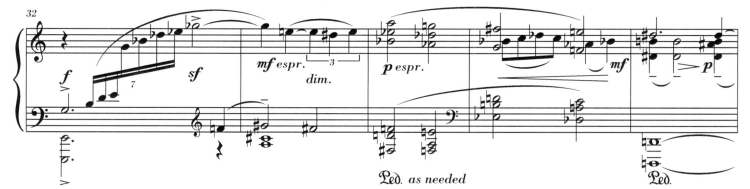

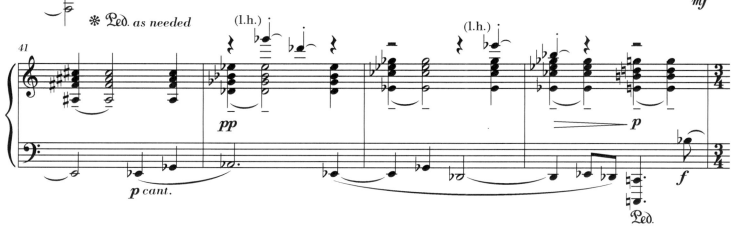

Poco meno mosso

$\quad$ = 96 *la sopra voce cantabile*

Più maestoso ♩ = 92

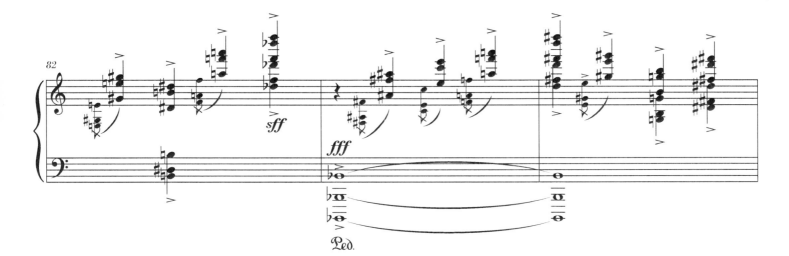

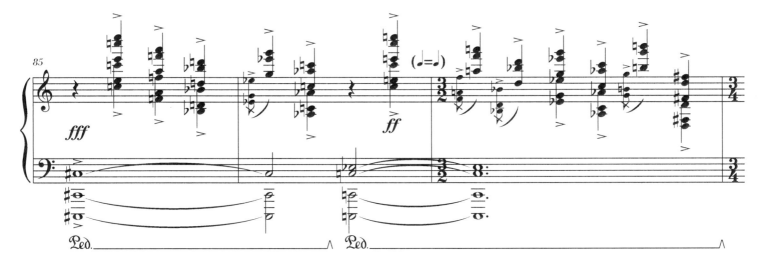

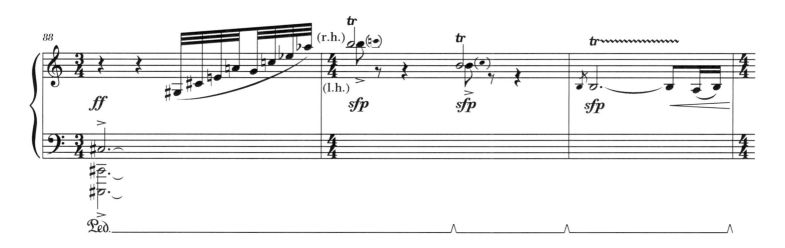

Freely, poco meno mosso
♩ = 80

Adagio, sostenuto
♩ = 48

don't drag

freely

rit.

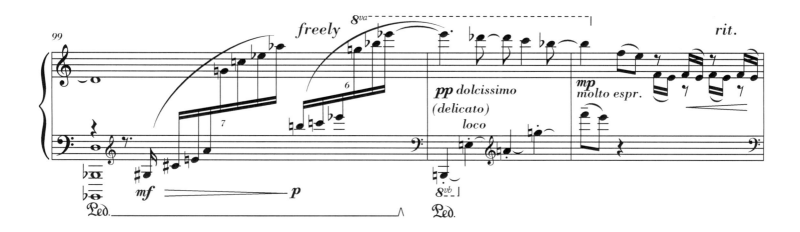

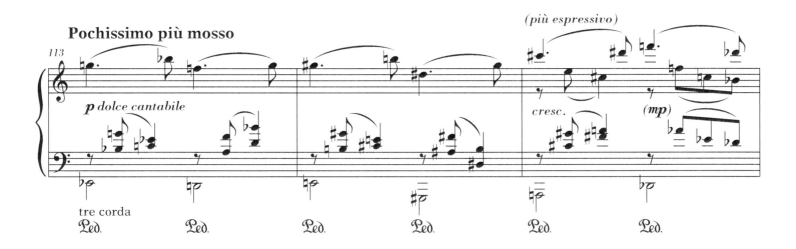

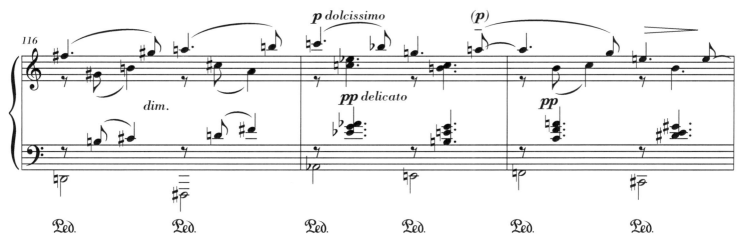

Con moto, un poco misterioso ♩ = 96

Leggiero ♩. = 96 *(flowing)*

rit.

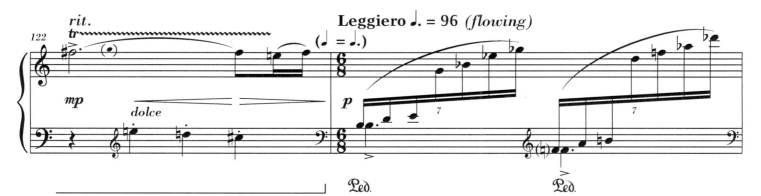

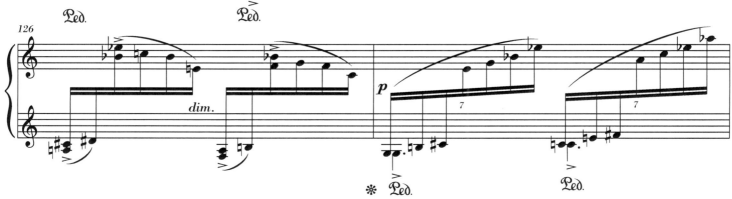

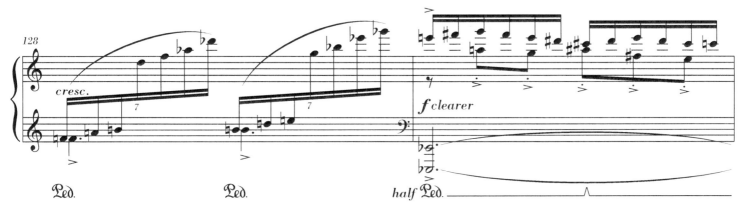

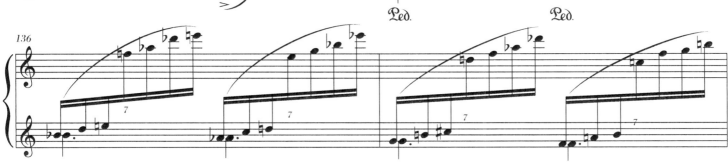

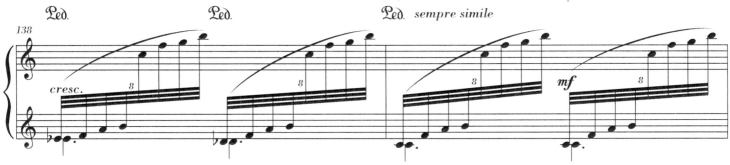

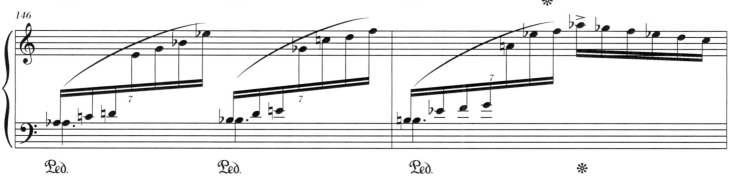

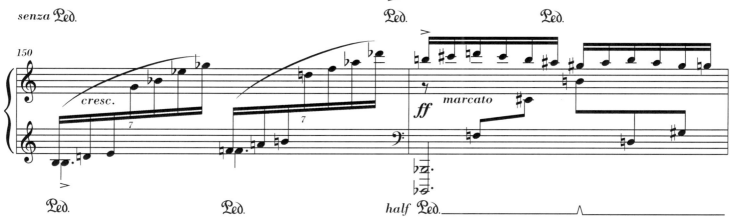

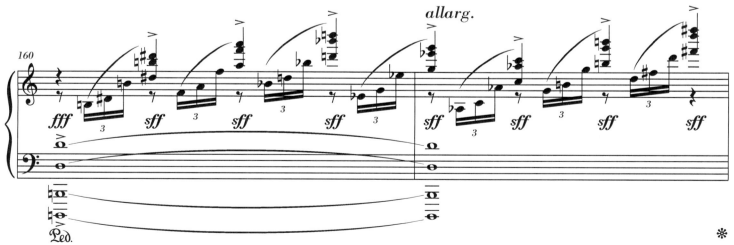

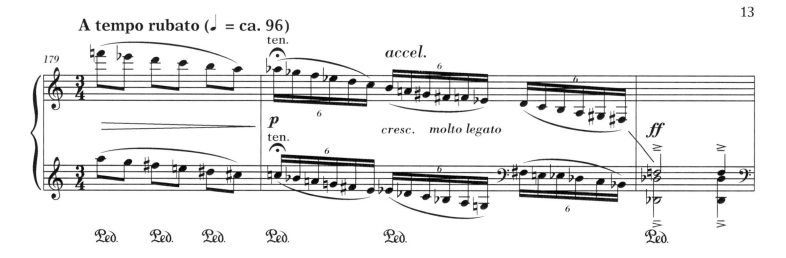

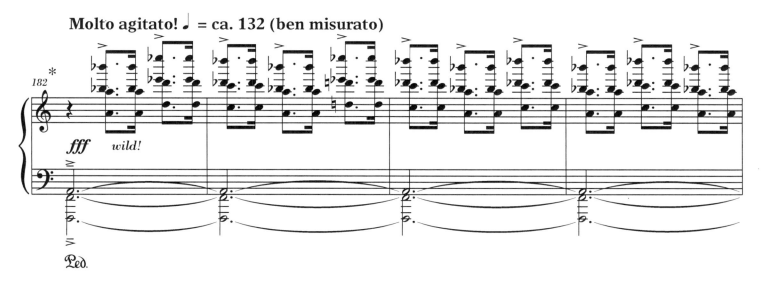

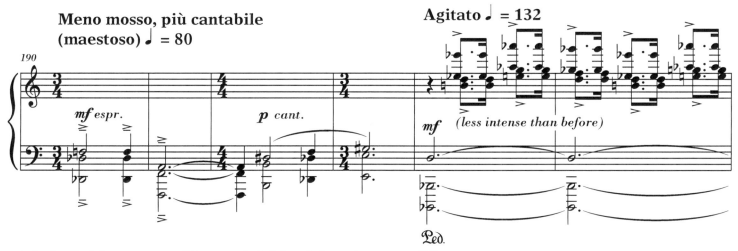

*: Ossia: Omit bottom note of F octave in left hand through measure 186.

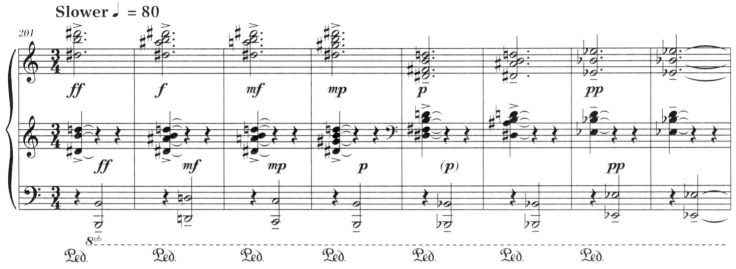

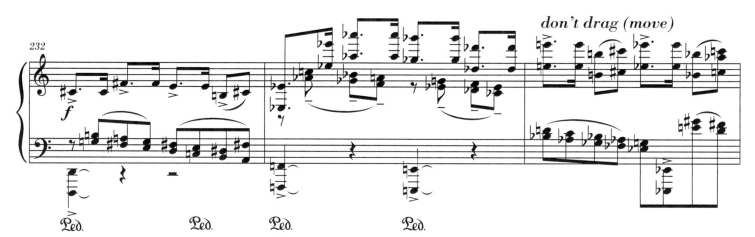

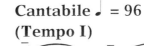

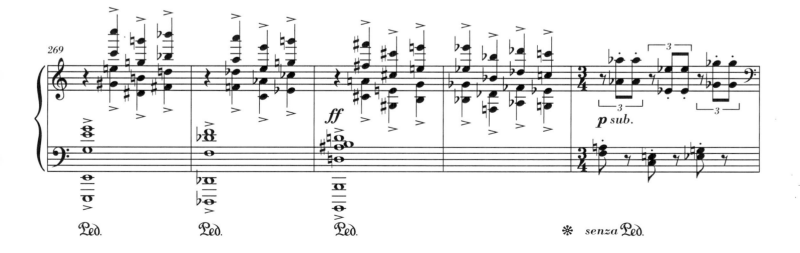

Maestoso ♩ = 72
(Tempo primo)

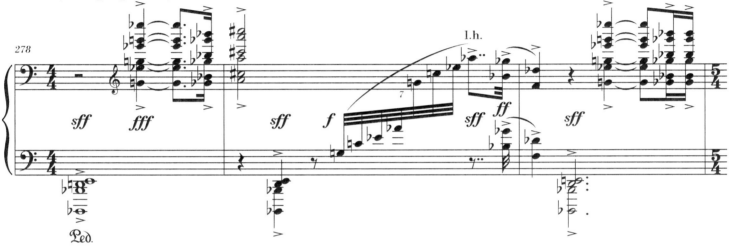

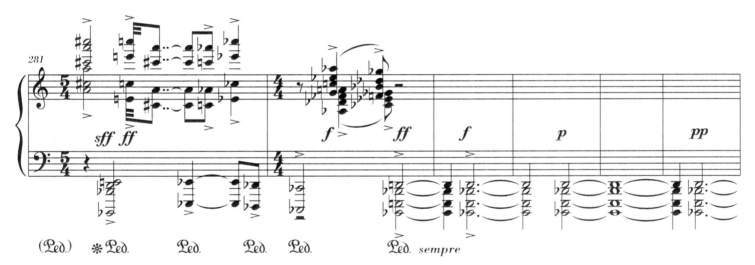

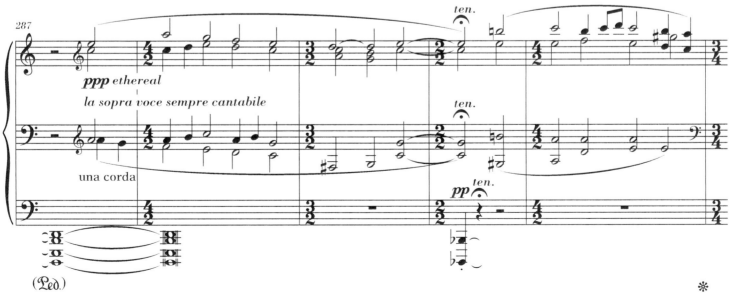

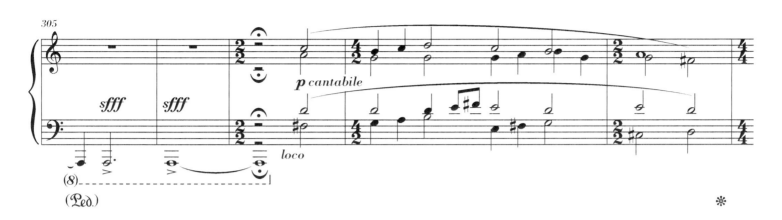

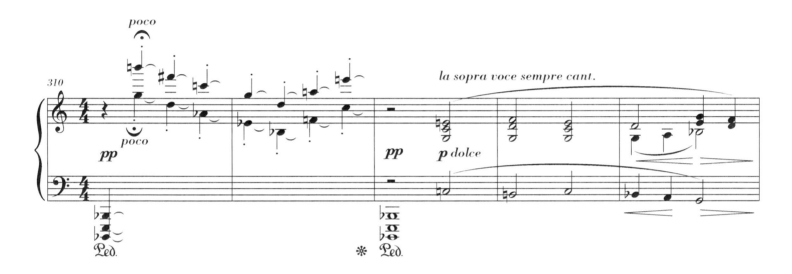

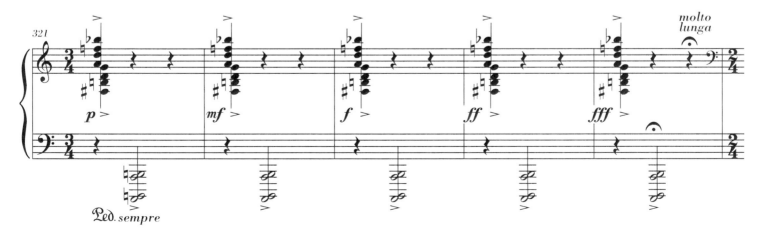

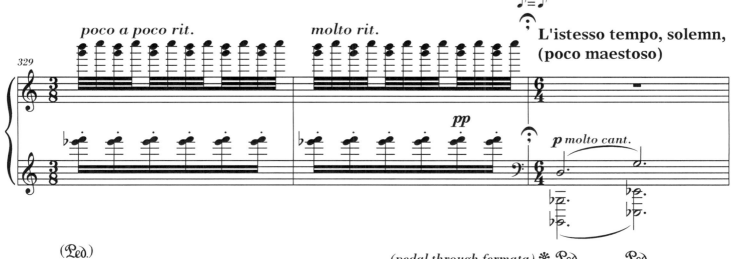

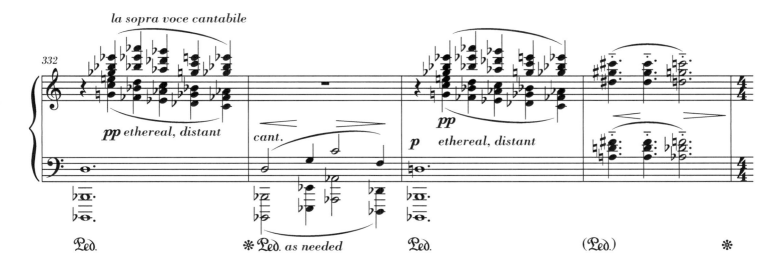